Piano • Vocal • Guitar

Best of LOS LOBOS

Cover photo © Corbis/ Pete Souza

ISBN 978-1-4584-1695-7

HAL•LEONARD®
CORPORATION
7777 W. BLUEMOUND RD. P.O. BOX 13819 MILWAUKEE, WI 53213

Visit Hal Leonard Online at
www.halleonard.com

BILLY

Words and Music by
BOB DYLAN

Moderate Tejano groove

There's

guns a - cross __ the riv _ er aim _ in' at _____ ya.
Camp - in' out __ all night __ on the __ be - ren _ da.

Law - man on __ your trail, __ he'd like to catch __
Deal - in' cards _ 'til dawn __ in the ha - ci -

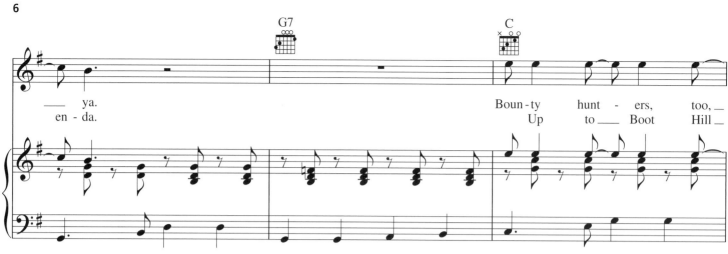

Play - in' 'round __ with some __ sweet, sweet __ se - ño - ri - ta.

In - to her __ dark hall -

- way she __ will lead __ ya.

In __

__ some lone - some shad - ows she will greet __ ya.

Oh, Bil - ly, you're so far a - way from home.

Instrumental solo ad lib.

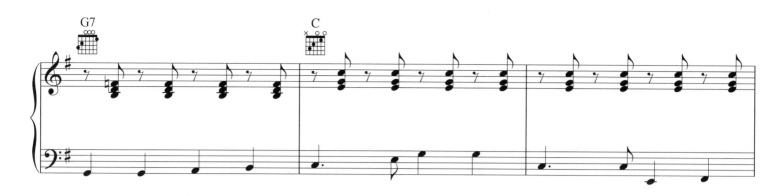

COME ON LET'S GO

Words and Music by
RITCHIE VALENS

DON'T WORRY BABY

Written by CESAR ROSAS,
LOUIS PEREZ and T-BONE BURNETT

Fast Blues Shuffle

Stand-in' there by the win - dow
- steps

star - in' out at the night, ___ you've got so man - y
steal - in' 'cross ___ the floor. ___ You picked up the re-

trou - bles ___ on your ner - vous mind. ___
ceiv - er, ___ you did - n't know what for. ___

But don't wor - ry, ba - by, it's gon - na work out fine. ___
Then you saw a shad - ow ___ step - pin' through the door. ___

B7

Em

You heard the sound of foot -

Well, don't wor - ry,

ba - by,   what   the   world   may   bring. __

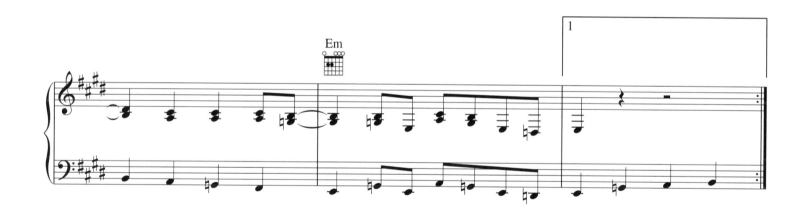

Stand-in' there by the win - dow

- in'

star - in' out at the night

and he could - n't sleep.

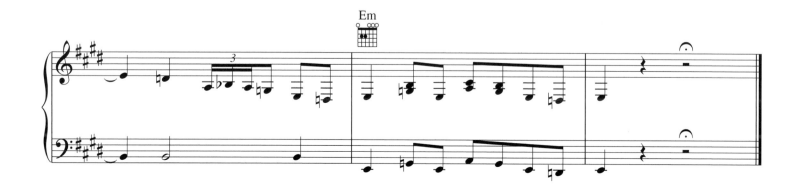

LA BAMBA

By RITCHIE VALENS

GUANTANAMERA

Written by DAVID HIDALGO
and LOUIS PEREZ

KIKO AND THE LAVENDER MOON

Written by DAVID HIDALGO
and LOUIS PEREZ

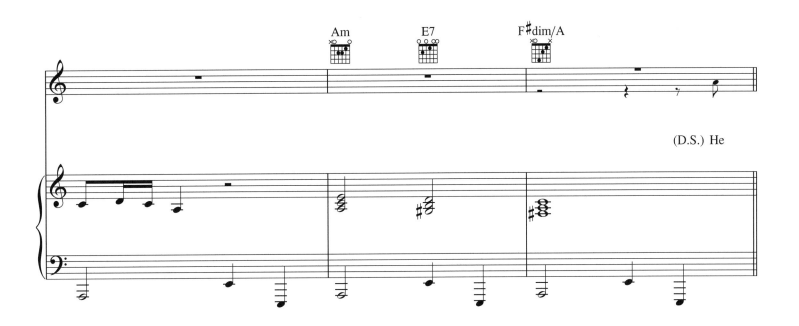

(D.S.) He

plays ___ and plays, ___ still play - in' till he goes off to sleep. ___
Dance ___ and dance, ___ still danc - in' till he goes off to sleep. ___

D.S. al Coda

he dreams, ___ Ki - ko and the lav - en - der moon. ___

MAS Y MAS

Written by DAVID HIDALGO
and LOUIS PEREZ

Moderately fast

Let's ___ go, mi chu - la, come ___
___ go, bai - lan - do, no -

___ on out with me. We can throw a chang - la till half pa - san - do three.
- che's look - in' fine. Jump in - to the ca - rro, ___ drink a bunch of wine.

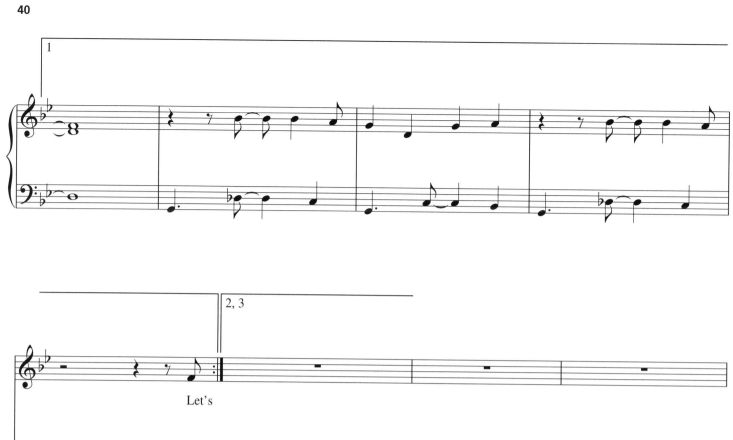

Let's

To Coda ⊕

D.S. al Coda
(take 2nd ending)

CODA
⊕

A MATTER OF TIME

Written by DAVID HIDALGO
and LOUIS PEREZ

ONE TIME, ONE NIGHT

Written by DAVID HIDALGO
and LOUIS PEREZ

Instrumental solo ad lib.

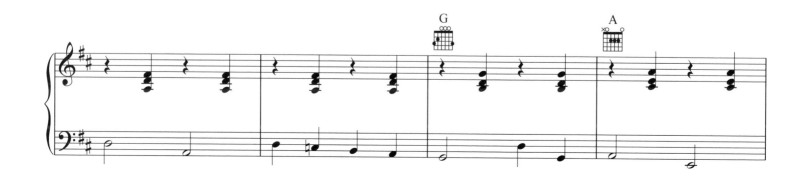

The sun - light plays — up - on —

— my — win - dow - pane. —

I

wake up to — a world — that's still — the same. —

SAINT BEHIND THE GLASS

Written by DAVID HIDALGO
and LOUIS PEREZ

Moderately fast

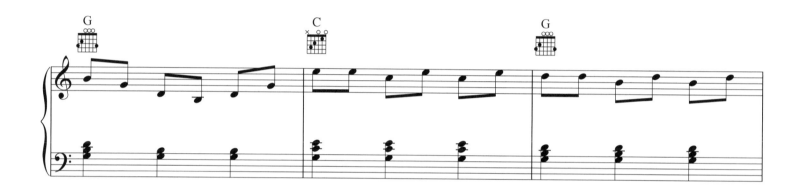

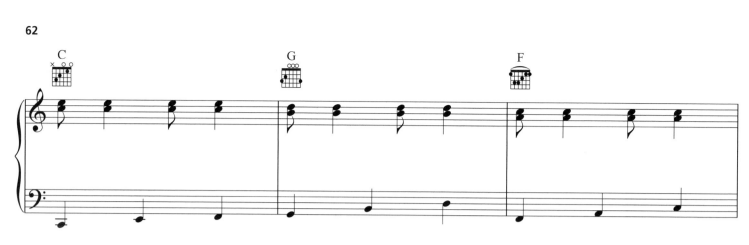

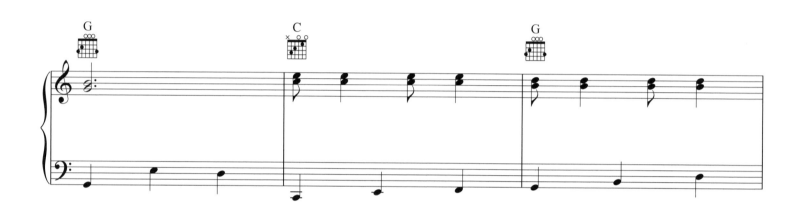

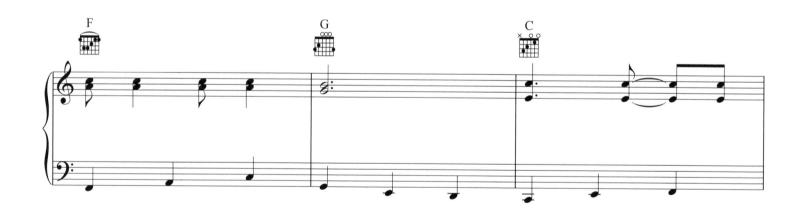

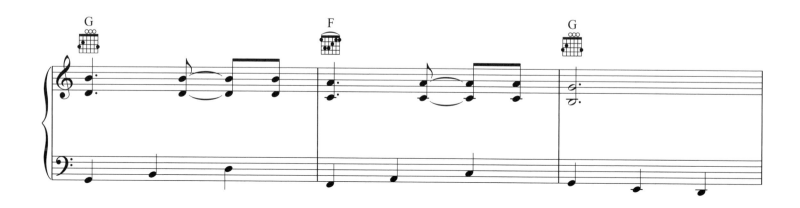

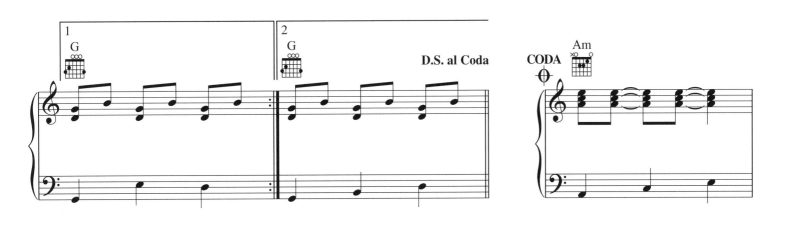

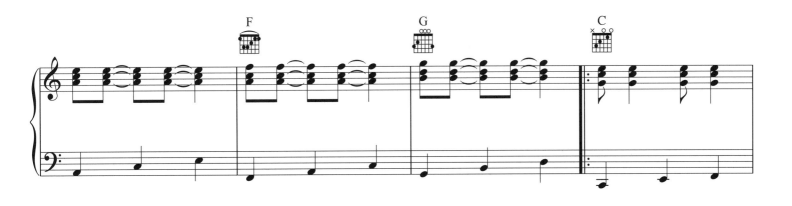

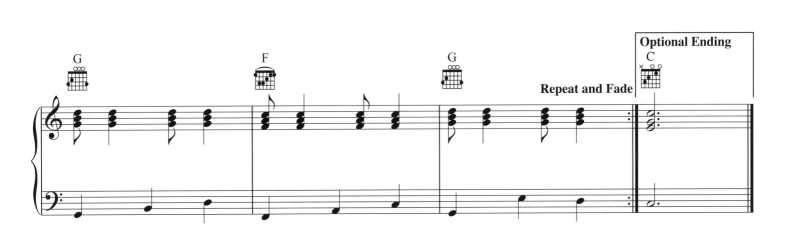

SHAKIN' SHAKIN' SHAKES

Written by CESAR ROSAS
and T-BONE BURNETT

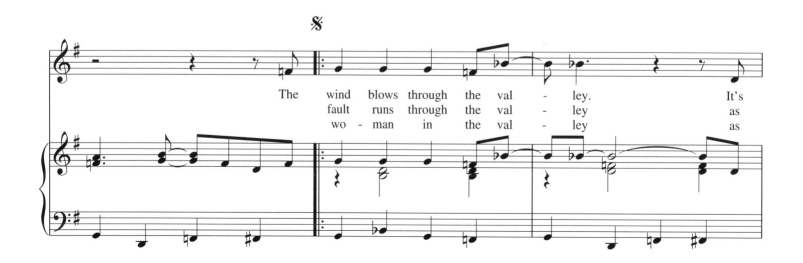

The wind blows through the val - ley. It's
fault runs through the val - ley as
wo - man in the val - ley as

CODA

Shak - in' and shak - in' and shakes.

Shak - in' and shak - in' and shakes. Shak - in' it shak - in' it

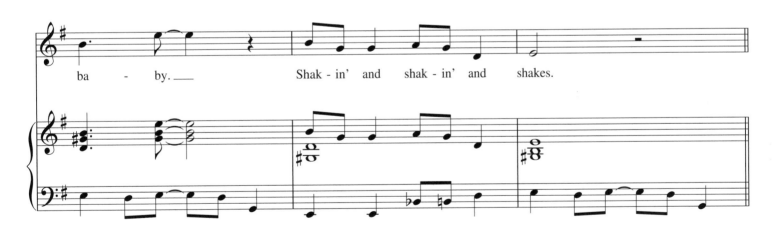

ba - by. Shak - in' and shak - in' and shakes.

Repeat and Fade

Optional Ending

Instrumental solo ad lib.

THAT TRAIN DON'T STOP HERE

Written by LEROY PRESTON
and CESAR ROSAS

Moderate Swing

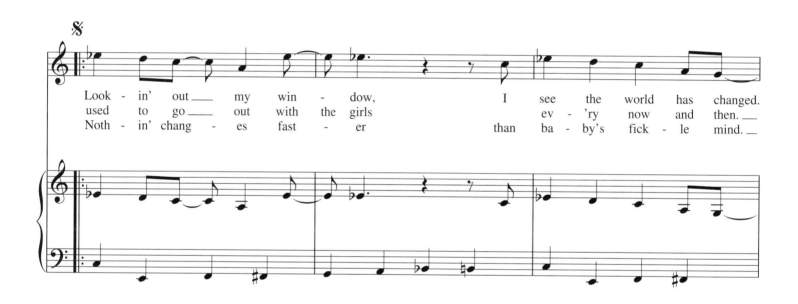

Look - in' out ___ my win - dow, I see the world has changed.
used to go ___ out with the girls ev - 'ry now and then. ___
Noth - in' chang - es fast - er than ba - by's fick - le mind. ___

___ The sun won't rise this morn - in' 'cause my
___ She al - ways came home ear - ly. We'd
___ I know she's lov - in' some - one

72

She ran out through the back ___ door,

scream - in' in the night. ___ She said I was ___ the dev -

- il. I did - n't ev - er treat her right. ___ The

WAKE UP DOLORES

Written by DAVID HIDALGO
and LOUIS PEREZ

Moderate swampy groove

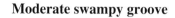

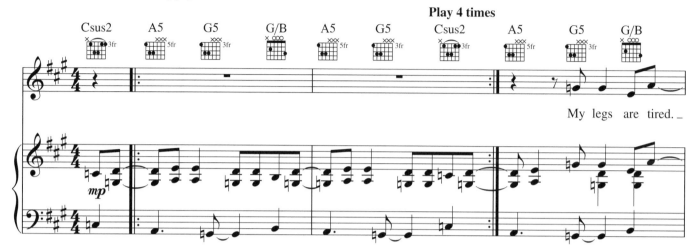

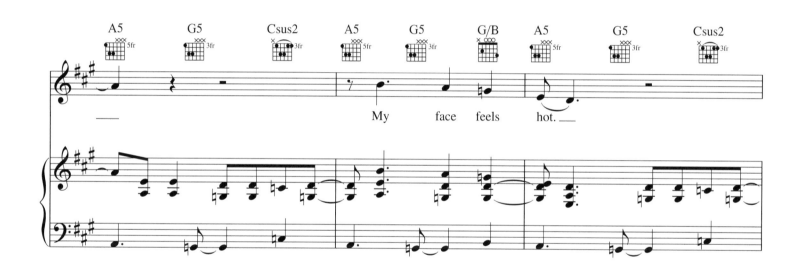

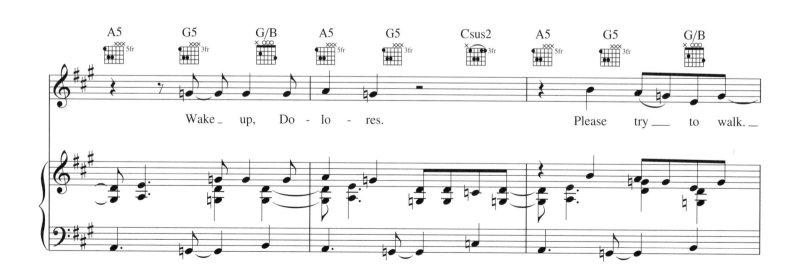

WILL THE WOLF SURVIVE?

Written by DAVID HIDALGO
and LOUIS PEREZ

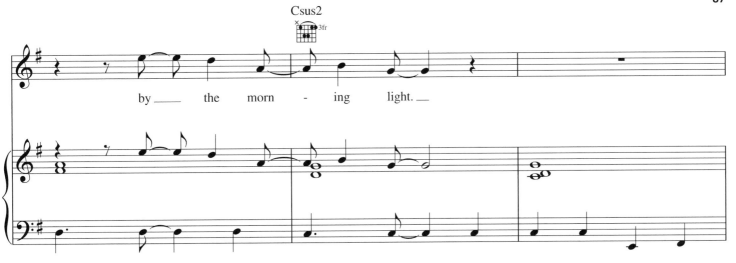

by _____ the morn - ing light. _____

Instrumental solo ad lib.

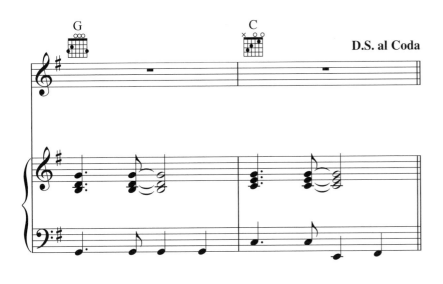

D.S. al Coda

CODA

Will the wolf _____ sur - vive? _____

Will the wolf __ sur - vive? _____

YO CANTO

Written by CESAR ROSAS

Le can - to a mi pa -
(2.)Tam - bien a mis ba -

- tria,   le can - to a mi gen - te _____
- rrios,   y a to - dos los va - tos _____

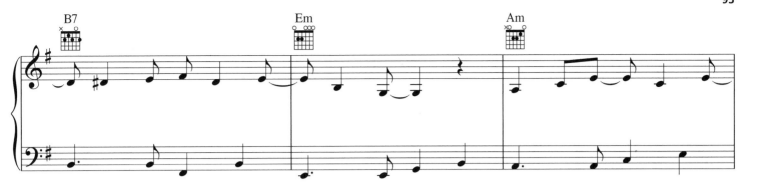

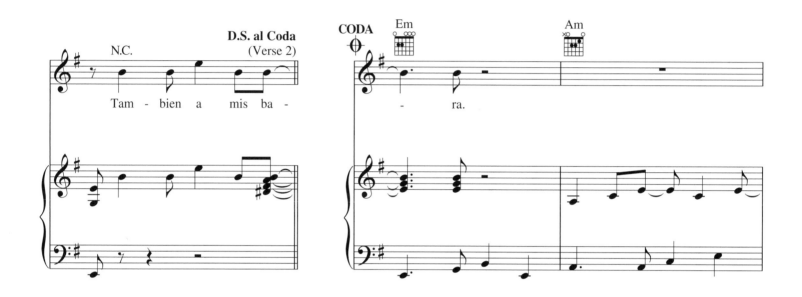

Tam - bien a mis ba - - ra.

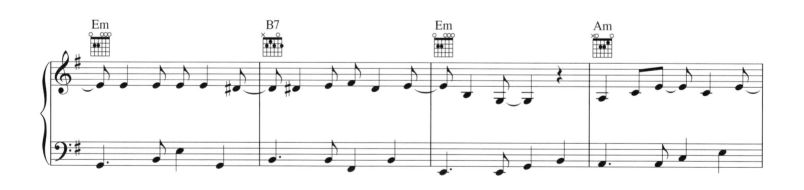

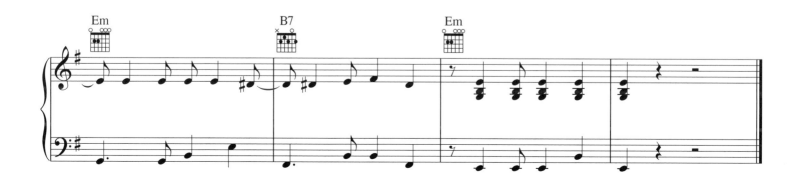